Tat

- Our Talks
- What's the Point?
- You Hurt Them
- Can't Love Anymore
- Let Me Leave
- What Do I Mean to You?
- Worth It
- You Fear You
- You Created This Heartbreak
- Greener Side of The Grass
- Anger and Hate
- Falling Apart
- That Moment
- Sinner
- Neglected
- This Might Keep Me Up at Night Unless I Write It Down
- You Played Me
- Not Good Enough
- Confessions
- Leave Me Alone
- Your Loss
- Blame on Me
- Stronger
- Crippled
- Take Me for Granted
- I Need Someone
- Poison
- I Don't Fit

Nylese Levin

Our Talks

I am not mad, nor do I feel hatred for how we departed
I just wish I can feel loved again
Our multiple talks that kept us up when the sun went down
We talked about our future
A wedding, children the white picket fence
We talked about our careers
You would always mention a life of happiness
And that's what I wanted
The days I could just talk to you
Talk about my life
Talk about my pain
You listened
I listened
But one day,
We stopped having our talks
And we stopped listening

What's the Point?

The point is, I opened up
I poured my heart out like a glass of lemonade on a hot sunny day
And you destroyed it
After years of being alone; after years of building this wall
I knocked it down for you in seconds
After years of needing no one
I somehow cannot survive without you
And I don't have the strength to build my walls back up
So now I'm broken, alone, and vulnerable
You left me with an open wound so everyone can stab it
I am feeble
You wanted me to open up
Am I too much to handle?
Or did you know you would mishandle me?
If you were going to destroy me, why not at least warn me?

The point is, I OPENED UP
I opened up because I wanted love
I opened up because I needed trust
I opened up because you told me to
You reassured me that you wouldn't leave
And you did

So, what's the point?

You Hurt them

When a person tells you that you hurt them
You don't get to decide that you didn't
You can't say that their feelings are don't matter
All because you interpreted their hurt another way
What you see as attention seeking was a heartbreak
When they cried
You lied and said it was their fault
When all they wanted was a hug
You departed and told them to grow a pair.
When they gave you their all,
You took it
Left them in the winds with nothing to survive on
You feasted like a family on thanksgiving
And you didn't even throw them a bone
When they vented and told you being left alone was their worst fear
You made them face their fears head on and no you weren't doing that to help them move on
You just wanted to hurt them
As if your reputation was worth more than their feelings
You once told them you loved them
And now at night they wonder if you really meant it

Can't Love Anymore

I thought I loved you
And I mean YOU, not the thought of you
But you were a lie
You lied about your very existence in my life
And when I looked into your eyes,
I saw the cries of a dying little boy
A dying little boy that wanted to drag me in his hole
The hole of deep depression
No progression in life whatsoever
You wanted to love me, just not enough
I told you i'd give you my heart just to repair yours
It was my fault
I didn't even make you earn it, nor did I make you pay
I gave
And I gave
And that was my mistake
I gave and I prayed
Now when you look into my eyes, all you see is the cries of a dying little girl
Don't stand too close or I'll drag you, down into my deep hole of depression
Only I can climb out
My happiness is gone
I'm the prey the dominant feasts on
I'm in this hole where I belong
Stay away

Let Me Leave

Your logic is
You won't leave me, but you won't treat me right
You say you love me to my face,
Then stab me in the back when I turn away.
You're selfish and cruel.
What's worse is that you hurt me, and you know it, but you don't care or when you hurt me without even knowing.
You caused me so much pain and now things won't ever be the same
I let you use me and drag my name
But now, it's your turn to feel this pain
You don't love me, so you won't be mad if I leave
You pull me at the collar and choke me
You don't love me, but you won't let me leave.

What do I mean to you?

What do I mean to you?
Do you love me?
Do you like me?
Do you hate me?
Do you despise me?
Am I worth enough for you to envy me?

What do I mean to you?
I look into your eyes and they no longer spark when you look into mine

You use me as a puzzle piece
You move me to get ahead in the game
You don't want to see me happy unless its with your permission
Unless you approve

And WHAT do you approve of?
You don't want me to move on
You don't want me happy
You don't want me to succeed
You don't want to marry me
You don't want someone else to love me and appreciate me

You just want to use and abuse me and break me till the point of no return
You just want me to be a damsel in distress so you can save me

You're the reason I need saving
It's you
I need to be saved because of you
I NEED TO BE SAVED BECAUSE OF YOU
So,

What
Do
I
Mean
To you?

Worth it

When you love someone,
You don't treat them bad
They should have all of your honesty
Because that's when the love is pure
And when they're feeling sad, it's your job to pick up the slack
Diamonds and pearls isn't giving someone the world
If their world is, you

Let them inside
Be sweet and kind
Put your pride aside
Life isn't perfect
But with your loved one, it'll be worth it
Sacrifices are perfectly normal
Building a love inside that'll never be defined
It's not perfect, it's worth it.

You Fear You

My mind is the home I'm trapped in
Where I never seem to win
They say to cut off all the things that hurt you
But what if that very thing is you?
You tell everyone that you're happy, but you know that's not true
Blaming no one but you.
Hating yourself for getting this deep into depression
Some moments are lessons that feel like a death sentence
That feel like the electric chair
Questioning if this is fair
You vs. You
Who will win?
Who will be the last one standing in the end?
Battle to the death
You'll have to kill yourself and you'll have to die
Seeing the murderer in the mirror
You're someone you fear.
It's you

You Created This Heartbreak

I gave my all to someone who couldn't give me a dime
Invested all my time and now it's time for you to pay
I've been waiting to hear the kind words you used to say
I could barely sleep without your face in my head
I could still feel your warmth in my bed
I think you're deaf sometimes because you can't hear
You listen to my words, but you don't feel my pain
You're never there to celebrate my gains
You left me feeling ashamed, yet again
All the hours I spent building a future that you never saw
You're the cause for this heartbreak
Now I'll never be the same.

Greener Side of the Grass

It hurts my heart that I can't get you off my mind.
Trying to move on but it feels like I'm running out of time
I'm just trying to survive
I'm mad at myself for letting you in
I didn't need to tell you a thing
Remember how you said that you'd get me a ring?
But for what?
Your promises are empty, and you leave me with no sympathy
You leave me feeling half empty
You leave me hurting myself because even now, I don't need me.
You came into my life and now all I want is you
I'm mad at myself but I'm mad at you too
How could you leave me?
You said that you need me
Then you tossed me aside like I was trash
I just wanted to be on the greener side of the grass.

Anger And Hate

The world is full of anger and hate
So of course, I'm going to smile my pain away
And every time I try, I can't
I'm losing my strength everyday
I can't fight no more
The pain is too much to bare
My heart is breaking, and no one cares
My cuts are getting deeper everyday

The world is full of anger and hate
So, if I'm made out to be the bad guy for loving myself,
So be it!
I'm a light bringer
Because there's nobody else who is going to love me like I love myself.
And no one is going to have my back
As a light bringer, I'm cold as ice
Call me Lucifer because I swear, I don't think twice.
I love myself and that feeling is just right.
I got tired of getting stepped on
Now I'm the one stepping
I'm the one moving up
I'm the one with all this self-love
I'm the one that no longer needs a hug or a pep talk

I'll bring myself up in this world of anger and hate
And I dare anyone to take something off my plate.

Falling Apart

Sometimes I feel empty
Get mad when people show me sympathy
I can't fight it anymore
Think I'm losing my own soul
Every day I feel completely alone
Feeling dumb for letting anybody in
They throw you away when you're worthless to them
You want to cry but don't have any more tears
Everything's falling apart in your bare hands
And you fear you're the one to blame
Threw yourself in the shadows
Drowned yourself in pity

Lost love
Lost hope
Lost fun
Standing on the sidelines
In a field you created…

That Moment

Hits you just at the right moment
Hits you different at night
The right moment of your happiness
The right moment of your success
Confronts you at your worst
Never lives to see your best
Depression goes to work and it's not a nine to five
Wondering why are you still alive?
If time isn't on your side
No one to build with
You don't even have yourself
It hits you just at the right moment
That moment of self-pity
That moment where you already wished you were gone
Now you're hurt
Can't love yourself if you don't know your worth
Now your brain and your heart are at work
Creating a hurt that you didn't even know existed
This is just the start.
Can you even make it to the finish?

Sinner

Sometimes the people I love can't help me
Sometimes I feel like my life is not healthy
No one understands the pain
They just underestimate me for their gain
Life was never easy
The simplicity is deceiving
In my life, I'm retreating
The walls are glooming
The shores are dooming
The sky is no longer blue
The world has no clue
Distractions, attractions
Constantly on a run
Leaving everyone wondering where is the joy?
Turning to violence because my wars are not won
In the dark because my sun has not shunned
Treating everyday like it's my last
Can never leave yesterday in the past
Trying to forget my mistakes
Trying to forget what has been done
The right and wrong can never get along
The sins of my sins will always win.

Neglected

I wasn't born this way
With the voices in my head telling me it's not going to be okay
With a shattered mirror that only shows my depression
With the dark clouds that ruin all my happiness
With the sight to see every flaw within.

I wasn't born this way
I wasn't born with hate or rage
I wasn't born feeling insane
I wasn't born with the blessing of knowing self-love
I wasn't born with tears in my eyes
Or fear in my heart

I wasn't born to feel hurt
Or to feel rejected and neglected

I wasn't born to feel at a loss
But I am this way now

So, what do I do?
Do I run or do I let it be?
What's my legacy?

Planting seeds in a garden no one will ever see
Is this the end of the happy me?
Was I born to be happy?
Who took that from me?
Who took away my smile and replaced it with anger?

Who took away my joy and made me lonely?
Who made me hate **ME?**
Who made me crazy?

This might keep me up at night unless I write it down

I'm up every night and not willingly
But forced
And even though it's my own body, it has a mind of its own
And everyone says they love me
But somehow, I still feel alone
And even though I work hard, I keep on failing
"do good and good will come to you"
Well, I've been doing good my whole life and still feel like a fool
I've been doing good and nothing good has come back
I've been beaten and thrown away
"one man's trash is another man's treasure"
No one wants a piece of coal
I'm no good
Not even for society
I run away just to be out of breath because I want to feel something other than tired
Other than sad
Other than alone
I want to feel warmth
And not from my hot shower
Or a blanket
But from another person's soul.

And this is what keeps me up at night
But instead, I'll tell you that I'm just not tired
When in fact, im quite exhausted
I'm tired internally and externally
Im tired in all three states
Physically, emotionally and mentally

But can you help me?
No
And that's fine. I can't blame you. I can't even beg you to stay
You want to leave, then be gone
No one stays but me
And I don't even want me here.

You played me

I don't want to memorize your face or your good grace
After you disgraced me and my name
We talked about the things closest to my heart
Yet you still had the audacity to rip it all apart
Maybe I gave you the ingredients
I wasn't expecting you to cook it up
Or burn it up
You didn't even clean up, you just walked out the kitchen
Never even reminiscing about all the good things I gave you
How I never shamed you or blamed you
You took me for granted
Planted the seed in my brain that you were the one for me
You didn't love me
You were just jealous
An envious baby!
Maybe that's the reason why you played me.

Not Good Enough

People tell me they want the best for me
I guess that's nothing new
I've always wanted the best for me too
But they second guess my ability
Which interferes with my capability
Now I'm sitting here alone and stranded
How did I get here and why am I empty handed?
I want to blame someone, but I can't find the bandit
I wanna build my wall up and keep everyone out
But I carve a hole because when I'm alone, I don't feel whole
I need someone to knock on my door even if I'm not home
But no one ever seen my "welcome" mat
I guess my house is too far in the back or it's just not enough to grab the reader's attention
Sorry I wasn't built to be your kind of beauty
But I am beautiful, and I am trying
And I will no longer be caught crying or comparing myself to what I think is best for me versus to what someone else wants me to be

Confessions

There's something you should know about
Something untold
Most may say I'm bold, but I have a few confessions
I cry when I'm alone
Yet I sit on a throne
I don't believe people when they say they love me
I don't trust words you say
And if I truly respect you, I won't let you see the worse in me, cause that's when you'll get mad at me.
I hate when people are mad at me
I let people hurt me and still give them my best
I come from a broken home but I won't let you know
I overthink at night and won't get a wink of sleep
I love too hard and that's why I get broken
I don't defend myself, I defend others
I'm treated as property
So, when I give you my all, please don't make me feel like it's a mistake
And I probably shouldn't blame you
I've been hurt so I'm always on my tippy toes
Any little thing sets me off
When people ask me what's wrong, I say nothing because I cannot explain this stress
When I cry, just know it's not about one thing, it's the world
When I cry in front of you, ill smile afterwards
I confess sometimes I hate myself
I look in the mirror in fear
Will I smile or frown?
Do I look nice or torn down?

I have glitter for a personality
But you won't know unless you get me open
I do things without thinking
And I confess I'm a sinner, but I can't talk about that
I confess that I try my hardest and still get let down
I walk outside with an upside-down frown
Not a smile!

Leave Me Alone!

When I ask to be alone, you don't leave me
But when I needed you to stay, you ran away
And when I cried out your name, you never came
I blamed myself
And for every time I looked in the mirror and felt ashamed
I think of throwing you into the flames
I've been burning and dying and crying meanwhile you've been lying
So why am I here?
Why am I here trying to piece myself together again?
I know when you come back, I'll let you in
And you'll destroy the very thing that I'm trying to protect
And that's my heart,
My mind,
My soul,
My body,
And anything else healthy within.

Your Loss

The blessed don't beef with the miserable
Which is why I don't pay you any mind
I gave you a chance and you blew it
You lost your only sense of mind
Now you're miserable
Lonely indeed, but I won't waste my time to try and help you
Because you'd turn into a thief
You'd try to steal what makes me, ME
Which is why I keep my distance and always stay calm
Can't get out of character for a person who doesn't even love themselves
I know my worth and I know my position in life
And I will not let you break me nor make me
And I won't give you the opportunity to know me twice!

Blame on Me

People say, stop making up lame excuses
That I'm useless
I need to become more ruthless
Don't forget where I come from
Grew up in the slums
That's why my heart is all numb
I need to think I come from the streets
Make sure my mistakes aren't left on repeat
Make sure my goals are complete
I never cheat, this life is just bittersweet
And one day I know it's going to take the best from me
I have to break down my wall.
I can't retreat
Some way I'm going to leave my mark on this concrete
And if my life ends up being incomplete
You can just put the blame on me

Stronger

People tell me my skin complexion is the best
I tell them I've seen better
They tell me my smile is so nice
I let them know about the whitest teeth I've seen
They tell me I'm beautiful
I show them a model
When they point out my "perfections," I downgrade myself
I call that neglecting my own pure soul
I thought I was building a wall to keep others out
But I was really just making sure I never get to see the bright light of the sunset
Nor hear the chirping of the sweet birds
Or the buzzing of the hardworking bees
I need to breathe
So, I knock down that wall and I instantly feel relief
I look in the mirror and I finally see what everyone has been telling me
My skin complexion is the best
It glows in the dark and shimmers when the sun comes out
My smile is so nice, it brightens a dark cave
I am beautiful
No need to look at magazines with the models because I am the best model that I have ever seen
Instead of building a wall, I should've built a bridge to get over the good I couldn't see within me.

Crippled

Rip away the very thing, the only thing
That puts a smile on my face
Break my trust
As if that was something I had a lot of
Give me a comfort zone
Then push me to my limits
You knew exactly what you were doing
I don't open up because getting my heart broke is something don't deserve
Keep to myself
Because there's no despair in being unaware of the drama that follows the devil
I won't listen because as soon as you ask for all of me, I'll easily open my mouth telling you that you can have me
Even though you don't deserve me
Especially since you desert me
I'm worth more than a hello and goodbye
I'm more sacred than your thoughts
And now I'm distraught in my depression
Wishing you weren't the one to teach me this lesson
Wishing you didn't treat me less than the people who say you're less than the working man
I shut down to keep the smile on your face
I don't protest
But you must know
Once you let me go, I'm not something you can repossess
You denied me the first time so there won't be a next
But like the fool that I am, I go against my own words to please you
I somehow convinced myself that I need you

I somehow convinced myself that my happiness is only genuine if it's given to me by the happiness of another human.
A human who tells me I'm unimportant
Not with words, but with actions making me wish I can go back to the past and change everything to mold myself a happy ever after
But happy endings are just factors in a fictional book
Therefore, my life will never be complete!

Take Me Granted

You took me
And rearranged my meaning
I used to actually care about what happens to me
Take everything I got and leave me dead
Cause I have nothing other than my soul
When I'm gone, donate my organs
I want to help someone at least once even if I don't get to see the smile on their face
And even then, their body can reject my organs
I'm just a bad fit
The world isn't meant to cooperate with who I am
I have to force myself to be who people want me to be
Then I finally got tired of holding up this wall
I let someone in and gave them my all
It's hard to see the real me, that's why I gave you glasses
But you sold them because money is more important than the beauty, I HAD within
Now I'm nothing and will forever be weak
Don't feed into my happiness because it's just a had been.

I Need Someone

I'm looking in the mirror and I'm feeling kind of distant
It feels like when I need someone
Everyone is missing
Everybody in my life is inconsistent
And every time I need something its inconvenient
But people need me for help
But I'm going crazy
I can't even help myself
How can you receive my help?
But can't be there for me
When I need you to help me when I'm going through things emotionally
You go back
You sit and relax
You don't care
When I call you never answer
And every time I come around you act like you're doing something better
And right now, im just feeling a little under the weather
Because I need somebody, but everybody wanted to do was leave me
I needed somebody but they never cared
But as soon as I'm gone, they're going to wish they remembered when I was here.

Poison

I don't think people invest their emotions into things as much as I do
But people that I called family walked out on me
People that I called friends and trusted with my words turned their backs and lied to me
This world is so corrupt
I don't even know what's right anymore
I'm drinking the poison that they're feeding me when I use to throw it down the drain
But this poison gives me the strength to spit in your face

This poison gives me the strength to know that I don't deserve the bad lectures
This poison gives me the strength to fight alone
This poison gives me the strength to move on and never be afraid
But this poison isn't my friend and when it wears off I'm alone and scared
That's why its poison

I Don't Fit

I have my walls built up from past hurt
Turned me into an introvert
Now people walk past me without even making eye contact
They must know I'm hurt
I don't fit
In this volcano of loneliness
I was only made to erupt
But I'll hold it in so I wont harm others
I don't want to be much of a bother
Feeling like a pimple on someone's back
Annoying
Hard to reach
Full of pain
But I've done so much for people
I've put my heart in situations that shouldn't have fazed me
I'm losing my mind and it's getting kind of crazy
I'm not a loser but I've been taking a bunch of L's
My lessons repeat like the S's in Mississippi
I just don't fit in!

Made in the USA
Columbia, SC
26 June 2025

59888580R00020